Bi[illegible]ning in t[illegible]days

Jackie Tidey

Contents

My Bird Book

I have made a bird book.

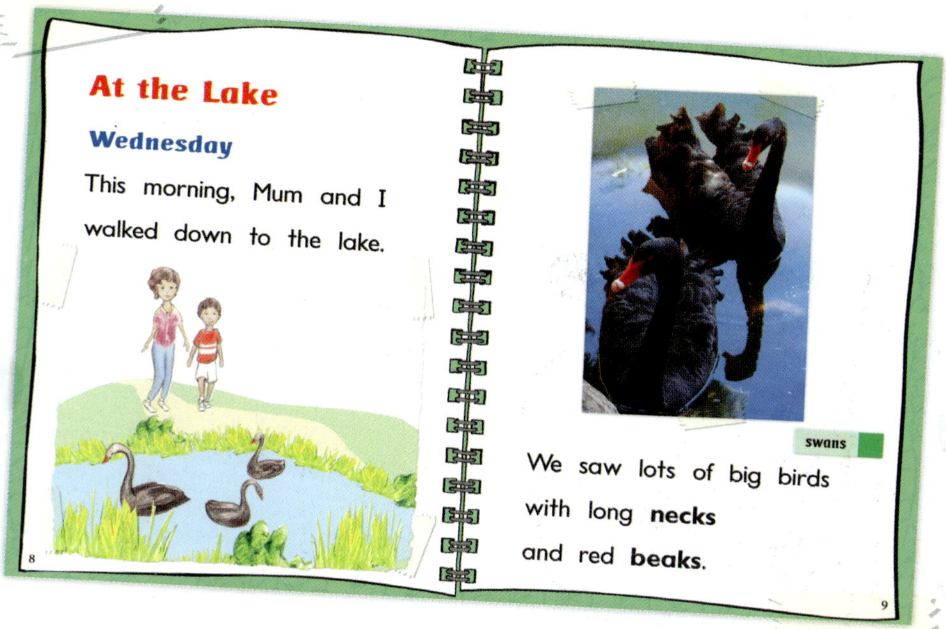
At the Lake

Wednesday

This morning, Mum and I walked down to the lake.

8

swans

We saw lots of big birds with long **necks** and red **beaks**.

9

My book has words and pictures of the birds I saw this week.

In Our Garden

Monday

Today, I saw two birds

in our garden.

doves

They had grey feathers.
Some of the feathers
had little white spots.

At the Beach

Tuesday

Mum and I had a picnic at the beach today.

Some birds ran up to us.

seagulls

They wanted some food.

We did not let them
have our food,
so they flew away.

At the Lake

Wednesday

This morning, Mum and I walked down to the lake.

swans

We saw lots of big birds with long **necks** and red **beaks**.

In the Street

Thursday

Mum and I saw
lots of birds in a tree.

They had green and blue
and red feathers.

The birds liked the seeds in the trees.

At the Bird Park

Friday

Dad came to the bird park with us today.

We went into a **bird-hide** at the park.

The bird-hide had windows
for us to look out
at the birds.

A white bird with long legs
flew over the water by us.

I saw lots of birds this week.

I like to look at birds
and draw them, too.

Glossary

beaks

bird-hide

necks